Dos and Don'ts
Business Etiquette and Professional Communication

Table of Contents

The single biggest problem in communication is the illusion that it has taken place.

— George Bernard Shaw

Chapter 1. Introduction

Welcome to a game-changing Special Report: "Dos and Don'ts: Business Etiquette and Professional Communication". Traverse a fascinating journey deep into the world of business interactions where every phrase you utter, and every gesture you make, could have a decisive impact on your professional prospects. Not your typical technical read, this upbeat report is laced with engaging anecdotes, easy-to-follow tips, and insightful case studies. From the first-time entrepreneur to the seasoned executive, everyone can find nugget of wisdom to refine their communication prowess. Don't miss this chance to redefine the way you conduct yourself professionally. Elevate your career, relationships, and stature within your industry just by mastering the art of effective business communication. This Special Report isn't just an investment, it's the secret ingredient to your professional success! One read and you'll wonder how you ever managed without it!

Chapter 2. Understanding Business Etiquette: A Prelude

Business etiquette forms the bedrock upon which businesses construct successful, harmonious relationships both internally and externally. Laymen often dismiss etiquette as an outmoded concept mostly relevant to social contexts. In truth, it is a veritable compass that guides people in correctly navigating the professional labyrinth, a labyrinth fraught with subtleties, unwritten rules, and potential missteps.

2.1. Understanding Business Etiquette

Business etiquette is more than knowing when to hold doors or chew with your mouth closed - these societal norms underpin the very fabric of how we relate, interact, and do business in today's interconnected world. But what is business etiquette precisely? It is an unwritten code of conduct guiding professional interactions, ensuring respect, and fostering workplace civility.

This mutual respect and civility go beyond the facade of superficial politeness. Business etiquette truly encapsulates the very philosophy of empathy, patience, and respect that help businesses grow hand-in-hand, promoting the all-important team-spirit, collaboration, and sense of belonging within an organization.

2.2. The Significance of Business Etiquette

With today's global business landscape growing increasingly complex and interrelated, the importance of understanding and practicing good business etiquette cannot be overstated. In communicating the right corporate culture, instilling professionalism, and fostering mutual respect, the role of business etiquette is paramount. It supports the confluence of diverse backgrounds, work styles, and communication approaches, ensuring all individuals feel valued and respected in their professional lives.

Good etiquette sets a stage for positive first impressions that influence subsequent interactions, showcases an understanding of others' needs, and communicates professionalism. Moreover, it can play a pivotal role in diffusing potentially tense situations and helping employees navigate controversial issues.

2.3. Elements of Business Etiquette

The modus operandi of business etiquette, though unwritten, holds its roots in common sense, with key elements being civility, professionalism, and respect. Nevertheless, a finer understanding can be subdivided into various components: teamwork and respect for colleagues; using the right tone and language; punctuality; grooming and professional attire; technological etiquette; etiquette in different business settings, and many more.

Teamwork and respect for colleagues - Business etiquette demonstrates respect for colleagues, fostering a collaborative, friendly, and harmonious working environment. It's about recognizing the strengths of others, supporting them in their activities, and minimizing conflicts.

Using the right tone and language - Verbal and written communication form the backbone of all professional dealings. Using the right language, tone, and diplomacy when dealing with clients or colleagues can be make-or-break in the professional world. Intelligent choice of words, maintaining a neutral tone, and avoiding offensive language are key business etiquette components.

Punctuality - Being on time shows respect for others' time and commitment levels, essential business etiquette facets.

Grooming and professional attire - Your appearance sets a precedent for people to judge your abilities and seriousness towards your work. Dressing appropriately for your workplace and maintaining good personal hygiene exhibit self-respect and respect for your work environment.

Technological etiquette - Technological advancements have created a new front for business etiquette to cover, with norms for e-communication, phone etiquettes, video conferencing, and social media behavior.

Etiquette in different business settings - Different contexts require different etiquette norms, whether they are informal gatherings, business meetings, or international business trips.

2.4. Conclusion

As Stapley rightly stated: "You can still be a business rebel. The entrepreneurial spirit thrives on out-the-box thinking. But it's a lot easier to play outside the lines when you have a good understanding of what the lines are." Business etiquette is the invisible cord that holds businesses together. In comprehending its essence, practitioners can look forward to transforming their professional lives, ensuring they resonate with respect and endear themselves to colleagues and associates, creating a win-win scenario for themselves and their organizations. A sound understating of business etiquette sets the groundwork for subsequent endeavors, whether in conversational etiquette, non-verbal communication, email etiquette, meeting etiquette, networking etiquette, social media etiquette, cross-cultural etiquette, or overcoming communication barriers.

Chapter 3. The Art of Conversational Etiquette in Business

Business, as the famous phrase suggests, is the art of conversation. However, this art shines brightest when paired with the awareness of conversational etiquette. Let's now delve deep into the realm of conversational etiquette in business, a mesmerizing universe where subtle cues and unsaid rules dominate the parlance.

3.1. The Importance of Communication Etiquette

Conversation underpins virtually every aspect of business operations, shaping our leadership legacies, influencing client relationships, and either promoting or stifling innovation within work environments. Clear, concise, respectful communication is the cornerstone of professional success. This ethic is not just confined to structured debates or board meetings but applies to every interaction that takes place within a professional arena, be it brief office corridor exchanges, canteen chit-chats, or virtual conference calls.

A sound grasp of professional communication is half knowledge and half art - understanding technical jargon and acing the elementary rules of conversation forms the "knowledge" part. The "art" is nuanced, requiring a keen understanding of cultural context, empathy, delegation, negotiation, and managing feedback.

3.2. Framing the Business Conversation: Context, Clarity, and Concision

To begin with, the context is central to business conversations. Like a promising sail in the vast ocean of dialogues, context guides the conversation, sets the tone, and eventually decides if the message has reached home or been lost to the mighty waves of confusion. To capture the essence of context, be mindful of your audience's knowledge and expectations, and align your style and content accordingly. A business meeting with a seasoned investor will require different language and topics than a casual brainstorming session with interns.

Clarity, the second spoke in our Watchwheel of Conversation, is the ability to express your thoughts and ideas in a manner that the audience can easily comprehend. Jargon plays an important role in business conversation. While specialized vocabulary may be a part of daily norm to one person, it may sound alien to another. Communicators must be deft at gauging their listeners' understanding and calibrating their message's complexity accordingly. Straightforward, accessible language entices both interest and comprehension.

The third crucial facet, concision, encapsulates the importance of being brief yet comprehensive. In a world of incessant deadlines and short attention spans, verbosity can be a lethal poison to productivity. Timing is the essence of good conversation - knowing what to say, how to say, and importantly, when to stop. Good communicators do not speak indefinitely, they share meaningful information and meet communication objectives in the most concise manner possible.

3.3. Body Language: Silent Swords of Conversation

Swiftly moving ahead, we arrive at the junction where etiquette meets body language, the interplay that complements verbal communication with nonverbal cues. Research indicates that non-verbal expressiveness contributes to nearly two-third of communication's total impact. Mastering the art of body language equates to finding the bridge between successful and unsuccessful conversations. It involves understanding the language of postures, the lore of gestures, the melody of facial expressions, and the rhythm of eye contact. Remember that your body speaks what your words may not. Be cautious of contradicting messages, where your verbal communication says one thing while your body language silently screams another.

3.4. Becoming an Active Listener

Conversations are a two-way street, wherein both speaking and listening are integral. Often overshadowed by the intense focus on 'speaking', listening is the underappreciated hero of communication etiquette that goes miles in building understanding, trust, and respect. Active listening, wherein the listener fully engages, understands, responds, and then remembers what's being said is an essential skill for succeeding in business. It shows respect, builds rapport, and encourages the speaker to elucidate, elaborate, and expound their ideas more freely.

3.5. Tackling Tough Conversations

Every business engagement, no matter how harmonious, sometimes necessitates tough conversations - disputes over contracts, conflicting ideas, dissatisfied clients, or performance-related feedback. Effective communicators, in such scenarios, tread the delicate line between being assertive without appearing abrasive. Be tactful, patient, and understanding. Lofty walls of defensiveness crumble through empathy, leading to conflict resolution and synergy.

3.6. The Final Word: Politeness Pays Off

Finally, remember that no matter the situation, maintaining politeness is quintessential. Courtesy is the fundamental underpinning of business relationships and connections. Even in moments of heated exchanges and intense disagreements, a respectful demeanor speaks volumes about your professionalism and composure.

Each business conversation is a unique dance of words, where the tempo is set by etiquette, rhythm defined by understanding, and choreography driven by intention and respect. Investing time and effort in mastering the art of conversational etiquette can pave the way for a delightful and productive expedition in the exhilarating world of business interactions. Hold the baton of professionalism, wear the shoes of respectfulness, and take the leap of faith into the arena of effective communication!

Chapter 4. Decoding Non-Verbal Communication: Body Language Matters

Commencing this chapter, I would like to quote a famous adage, "Actions speak louder than words." This saying encapsulates the essence of non-verbal communication in a nutshell. Non-verbal communication or more specifically, body language, contributes significantly towards your professional image and can often convey more than spoken words.

4.1. The Power of Non-verbal Communication

Contrary to popular belief, communication isn't just about the words that you utter. In fact, non-verbal communication, including body movements, facial expressions, eye contact, and posture, plays an integral role in the way your message is perceived. These non-verbal cues can reinforce or contradict the spoken words, making them an essential aspect of business communication.

Consider this: you're communicating a significant change in your company's operations to your subordinates. You are explaining the reasons in utter detail, but your facial expressions appear unconfident, and you're continuously fidgeting. Regardless of the articulation in your speech, your body language sends a completely different message – one of unease and doubt.

Hence, decoding body language not only helps in better understanding and interpretation of messages but also aids in controlling and correcting your physical behaviors unconsciously communicating your feelings or intentions.

4.2. Body Language: Types and Their Interpretations

Now let's delve deeper into the different types of non-verbal communication. Each type, if aptly used, can go a long way in ensuring your words are met with the impact they deserve.

Posture: The way you sit or stand plays a critical role in your interaction. An upright posture exudes confidence and attentiveness. In contrast, slumping, hunching, or leaning back signals disinterest or lack of enthusiasm.

Eye contact: Looking directly into someone's eyes during conversation signifies honesty and interest. Regular, but not continuous, eye contact communicates your attentiveness and respect for the listener.

Facial expressions: Your facial expressions are the windows to your feelings. Smiling showcases approachability and friendliness, while a furrowed brow can depict concentration or worry.

Gestures: Hand movements add emphasis to spoken words. Open-hand gestures signal openness and honesty, while excessive fidgeting could indicate nervousness or discomfort.

Space usage: Respect for personal space is crucial. Invasions of personal space can create discomfort, so maintaining an appropriate distance while communicating is necessary.

Touch: In a professional context, touch usually is limited to handshakes. A firm, confident handshake often leaves a powerful, lasting impression.

Silence: The pauses or silence can be used to emphasize the importance of a point, allow the listener to absorb information or act as a tool to handle tricky discussions.

Remember, these interpretations can vary based on context and culture and should only be used as a guideline rather than a strict rulebook.

4.3. The Art of Reading Body Language

Being able to read body language enhances your interpersonal skills as it aids in understanding unspoken issues, hidden emotions, or feelings. Here are some strategies to understand body language better:

1. **Look for Congruence**: If the verbal and non-verbal communication are not aligned, you need to probe further into the communicator's real feelings or intentions.

2. **Context Matters**: Always consider the context of the interaction. A crossed arm could mean defensiveness, but it could also mean that the person is simply feeling cold.

3. **Evaluate Cumulative Cues**: Rather than analyzing individual gestures, look for a pattern or cluster of behaviors for accurate interpretation.

4. **Trust your Instincts**: Your subconscious mind picks up and interprets body language cues even if you're not consciously aware of them. So, trusting your gut feeling can sometimes be the right way to decode body language.

4.4. Strategies to Improve Your Body Language

Improving body language involves becoming conscious of your non-verbal cues and working to align them with your verbal messages. Here are some strategies:

1. **Self-awareness and Practice**: Observe your gestures, facial expressions, posture, and other non-verbal cues. Practice in front of a mirror or record yourself while speaking to notice patterns.

2. **Adopt Power Poses**: Research indicates that adopting power poses (open, wide, and large postures) can boost your confidence levels.

3. **Improve Eye Contact**: Practice duration and quality of eye contact during conversations. Too little may portray disinterest, while too much may make the other person uncomfortable.

4. **Manage Nervous Habits**: Identify your nervous habits like fidgeting or toe-tapping, and work on controlling them.

5. **Imply Positivity**: Use positive gestures like smiling, nodding, and leaning slightly toward the speaker to show interest and understanding.

Remember, mastering non-verbal communication is not an overnight process. It requires continual learning, practice, and adjustments based on various factors like culture, setting, and personal comfort.

Wrapping up, decoding non-verbal communication or body language is a powerful tool in professional communication. Your ability to interpret and respond to non-verbal cues appropriately and control your body language can help you establish robust business relationships, lead more effectively, negotiate better, and create a more positive professional image. Cultivating these skills provides a critical edge in today's competitive business world.

Chapter 5. Email Etiquette: The Digital Letter of Professionalism

Indeed, in our digital world where the bulk of communication is conveyed through written text, mastering the art of email etiquette is of paramount importance. The significance of your message could easily be undone by a simple typographical error, a misused word, or a misunderstood intent. Even in the informal sea of cyberspace communication, your professionalism must shine through in your emails. So let's delve deeper.

5.1. The Basics: Structure and Style of Professional Emails

Professional emails can be categorized into three main parts: the subject, the body, and the closing. The subject should be precise, concise and correctly represent the content of your message. Avoid flippant or vague subjects. The body, the heart of your email, should start with a warm greeting, followed by your content neatly divided into clear, concise paragraphs. Don't forget a formal closing, even if your email is brief.

The general style of your email should emanate professionalism and respect. Remember, your email could be read by higher-ups or could be forwarded to other professionals. So always, err on the side of formality. Use grammatically correct sentences, proper capitalization, and avoid emoticons, abbreviations, or slang.

5.2. Addressing the Recipient Correctly

Careful consideration should be given to how you address your recipient. If you're writing to someone you don't personally know, or in all cases of first-time communication, use a formal salutation. When in doubt, always fall back on 'Dear [First Name]'. Never start your email with a generic 'Hello' or 'Hi'.

In case of multiple recipients, it's even more important to address everyone correctly, especially when there are people of various ranks involved. For larger groups, a 'Dear Team' or a 'Dear Colleagues' could work well. Respect each individual's title and gender. When unsure of the gender, use their full name.

5.3. Clear, Concise Content

Email is not the platform for verbose, long-winded letters. When writing, clarity and succinctness are highly valued. Before hitting send, ask yourself: "Can this be understood in 60 seconds or less?" Use bullet points or numbered lists for easier readability.

Ensure that you convey your intent properly. Emotion and tone can get lost or misconstrued in emails, creating confusion or, worse, confrontation. Stick to neutral language. Save your humor, irony, or sarcasm for face-to-face communication.

5.4. Importance of Proofreading

Simply put: proofread every email. Grammatical errors and spelling mistakes can undermine the weight of your message, distract your reader, and simply look unprofessional. Additionally, always double-check to ensure you're sending the email to the intended recipient/s and that all relevant documents are attached as necessary.

5.5. Timely Responses and Follow-Ups

Prompt responses demonstrate respect towards the sender's time and effort. In case a thorough response will take time, an acknowledgment email helps to keep communication flowing smoothly. However, beware of 'email ping-pong'. If an email thread goes beyond three replies without resolution, consider another mode of communication.

Following up is another crucial element of email etiquette. If you've not heard back within a reasonable timeframe, it's perfectly professional to resend your email or send a polite reminder. It communicates persistence and the importance of your agenda.

5.6. The Fine Art of CC, BCC and Reply All

These functions should be used judiciously to avoid spamming irrelevant recipients, inadvertently revealing sensitive email addresses, or excluding involved parties. Be very certain when to CC (carbon copy) or BCC (blind carbon copy) someone, and mindful when hitting 'Reply All'.

In conclusion, a well-crafted professional email is an asset not to be underestimated. With the principles laid out in this chapter, you're well on your way to mastering the digital letter of professionalism. Remember, email communication is about building relationships as much as it is about exchanging information; a skillful email can open doors, build rapport, and secure your professional reputation. Let your emails be a hallmark of your dedication, competence, and professionalism.

Chapter 6. Meeting Etiquette: Productivity in Politeness

The world of business is one where meetings are a commonplace. Each subsequent gathering becomes but an addition to countless others, set within glossy conference rooms or across shiny virtual platforms, each playing out their own tale of significant decisions and heated deliberations. However, far too often, the very spirit of these important congregations is shadowed by an overlooked element – meeting etiquette. When observed carefully and practiced religiously, meeting etiquette can harness distortions in the communication lines, improving the overall productivity and fostering an atmosphere of respect.

6.1. The Pre-Meeting Protocol

The journey to effective business meetings begins much earlier from the actual meeting time, within the realms of what's known as pre-meeting protocol. This primarily entails a well-structured meeting agenda, shared in advance to all the participants. An outline of the various subjects to be addressed, the schedule, expected attendees, and the outcomes you wish to achieve from the discussion... all of these crucial data points pave the way for a productive meeting.

First off, let's start with the timing. It is vital to schedule your meeting at a time that is suitable for all participants. This can get especially tricky with remote teams strewn across different time zones. Tools like World Time Buddy come in handy in such scenarios. Once the feasible slots are identified, ensure to keep the meeting succinct and time-bound.

Secondly, the role of a well-curated agenda cannot be understated. It ensures that the attendees come prepared and with a clear understanding of their own roles within the meeting. Specific goals should be outlined to maintain the meeting's focus and avoid it from turning into an aimless chatter. The more concise, specific and oriented towards the meeting objectives your agenda is, the more fruitful your meeting will be.

6.2. The Etiquette of Conducting the Meeting

The stage is set, agendas have been sent out, and the clock strikes the decided hour. The meetings are not just a simple exchange of words and ideas but a dance, a performance, where every step you take, every move you make reverberates through the ranks of the attendees.

Punctuality is an often mentioned, yet consistently violated tenet of the meeting decorum. Starting on time signals your respect for the other attendees' time and ensures the meeting adheres to its planned timeframe. If you're the moderator, make sure you arrive a few minutes early to set up, ensuring there are no technical glitches or last-minute hiccups.

Once the meeting commences, the role of active listening comes to play. Paying attention to what each speaker contributes constructs an atmosphere of mutual respect and facilitates constructive conversations. Discourage disruptive behaviors such as side conversations, frequent interruptions, or multitasking.

Another vital aspect is the facilitation of open dialogue. Encourage all participants to share their thoughts and ideas, creating a space for diverse perspectives. Ensure that credit is given where it's due and be conscious to moderate any dominating behaviors that might stifle the conversation.

6.3. Mastering the Art of Virtual Meeting Etiquette

In the digital era, punctuated with the rise of remote work, virtual meetings have become the new norm. The etiquette for virtual meetings derives from the same fundamental principles as face-to-face meetings but has a few unique stipulations.

Ensure that your surroundings are devoid of distracting elements. Keep yourself on mute when not speaking to avoid any background noise interfering with the meeting. Ensure your internet connection is stable and that your camera is turned on at all times during the meeting to foster a sense of connection.

Leap over the digital divide by taking time to engage with others, both formally and informally, making space for those casual, water-cooler-type conversations that build camaraderie. This helps in nurturing relationships within the team, thus bolstering more effective collaboration.

6.4. Reflecting Upon the Meeting: Post-Meeting Etiquette

As the meeting curtains draw to a close, it doesn't signal the end of the consideration for etiquette. A summary outlining the key points discussed, decisions taken and tasks assigned should be shared promptly after the meeting. A practice that proves to be massively beneficial and provides a quick reference guide to all the attendees.

Apart from the meeting minutes, another integral part is to request feedback. This allows for continuous improvement in the way meetings are being conducted, keeping them streamlined, engaging, and productive.

Business meetings, fundamentally a crucible of decision-making, get a complete transformation when attended with a refined sense of etiquette. It can be summed up nicely with a quote from Peter Drucker, a renowned management consultant, "Efficiency is doing things right; effectiveness is doing the right things", and in the context of corporate meetings, the 'right thing' is indeed polished meeting etiquette. Armed with these insights and strict adherence, your meetings are sure to transcend from being a mundane protocol to an influential platform facilitating cognizant discussions and impactful decisions. All while reinforcing the bedrock of professional respect and cooperation.

To conclude, professional conversations speak volumes about the overall image and successful trajectory of a business entity, resonating beyond the confines of the conference room, which is why it is absolutely essential to master the art of meeting etiquette: the cornerstone of productivity in politeness.

Chapter 7. Networking Etiquette: Building Relationships with Grace

Networking is a highly intricate art that requires one to grapple with a myriad of elements simultaneously – building robust ties, making a good impression, broaching the right topics, and gracefully navigating both formal and casual settings. The trick lies in approaching it with a clear set of guidelines and honing those social skills to a gleaming point where they seem second nature. This chapter aims to explore these guidelines in depth, offering you a roadmap to build productive relationships with elegance and grace.

7.1. Understanding the Importance of Networking

Networking essentially is the building block of professional relationships. It takes two fundamental forms: informal, casual interactions, and formal, strategized engagements. Regardless of the context, networking is becoming increasingly vital in today's highly connected, ebullient business fabric. It can open doors for opportunities, expand your understanding of your field, keep you up-to-date with trends and developments, and even establish your personal brand and reputation.

In this digital era, networking isn't limited to face-to-face encounters. The internet offers endless possibilities, from LinkedIn connections to clicks over Twitter and Emails. However, the core principles remain the same, and it's their effective application that garners success.

7.2. Crafting a Convincing Introduction

The first impression is a pivotal determinant of your networking success. It is during this crucial juncture that people form an image of who you are, what you represent, and how beneficial you can be. Therefore, it's essential to make the most of this brief window to craft a compelling, sincere, and confident introduction.

A strong introduction comprises your name, your current role, and your interests or passions. Ensure to strike a balance between professional and personal details—being just as open to discussing your love for hiking as your upcoming project. It shows that you're a multifaceted individual, thus more engaging.

7.3. Active Listening and No Interruptions

Being a good listener is a critical, yet often underrated, aspect of networking. Active listening involves genuine engagement with the speaker, responded with relevant comments, questions, or experiences. This encourages the other person to continue talking and sends the message that you respect their thoughts and opinions.

While it's compelling to jump in with your views or stories, it's prudent to refrain. Allow the other person to complete their thoughts—cut-offs are rude and shut down the conversation flow. In addition, make a conscious effort to maintain eye contact. It not only displays attentiveness but also helps retain speaker details.

7.4. Appropriate Use of Business Cards

Business cards have remained an enduring element of networking, even in our tech-driven age. They serve as a physical reminder of you for future reference. However, their use has to be tactful. Hand over your business card at an optimal moment during the conversation, preferably towards the end, or immediately after the other party expresses interest in contacting you.

Moreover, respect the business cards you receive. Take a moment to look over the information before placing it carefully in your wallet or cardholder. Treating others' business cards with care conveys respect and interest.

7.5. The Power of Follow-ups

The vitality of follow-ups can't be stressed enough. Following-up can be via an email, a social media message, a phone call, or even a text message. It not only shows that you valued the conversation but also solidifies your relationship with the contact. However, a balance is needed— too soon might come off as invasive, but too late and you risk seeming disinterested.

All said, networking isn't a one-off event but a constant process. Therefore, staying connected over time even without immediate needs portrays your genuine interest in the relationship rather than a transactional approach.

7.6. Balancing Personal and Professional Boundaries

Networking is undeniably blurred between the professional and personal realms, which is why it's vital to maintain a delicate balance. You must remain respectful, maintain professional language, and avoid controversial topics. At the same time, demonstrate warmth, stay open for friendships, and exhibit humility. This balance ensures that your networking relationships are on a sturdy and reliable foundation.

In conclusion, networking is an art that is as rewarding as it is challenging. By following the guidelines discussed and practicing them regularly, you can gracefully navigate networking seas, building not just relationships but potential partnerships and friendships that could impact your professional journey remarkably. Enjoy the networking journey, and soon enough, you'll grasp its rhythm, finding joy in the connections you build and the diversity you encounter.

Chapter 8. Social Media Etiquette: Professionalism in the Digital Age

In this flourishing age of digital communications, one might argue that social media has successfully bridged the virtual and physical world, crafting a unique tapestry of human connections. The interactive platforms of social networking channels such as Facebook, Twitter, Instagram, and LinkedIn have metamorphosized the professional landscape, offering unparalleled opportunities for global networking, recruitment, self-branding, and information sharing. But, as Peter Parker (aka Spiderman) learns from his dear Uncle Ben, "With great power, comes great responsibility", a dictum that firmly applies to the digital realm as well. It's time we dive deep into unraveling the unwritten playbook of social media etiquette within a professional context.

8.1. The Power of Perception on Social Media

On social platforms, you are what you post. Each shared article, comment, retweet, or like contributes to the mosaic that shapes your online persona. This digital portrayal supplies valuable insight for potential clients, employers, colleagues, or competitors. The rampant rise of cancel culture illustrates just how quickly a misplaced word could ignite plummeting reputations and lost opportunities.

Curate a consistent online identity that accurately mirrors your professional values, your work ethics, and expertise. Use these digital platforms as a voice of your personal brand; reflect upon what you want to represent and persistently reverberate that in every interaction. Mind your language, be respectful, shelve sarcasm or humor that could possibly misread, and respect the diversity of your online fraternity.

8.2. Privacy, Confidentiality, and Discretion

Understanding the boundary between public and private is potent. Private matters, including proprietary company information or sensitive client details, have no place on social platforms. Overexposure can often lead to less credibility. Many platforms come with nuanced privacy settings, enabling users to control content visibility - use them to your advantage.

In situations where the line between professional and personal blurs, exercise absolute discretion. It is absolutely inappropriate to air workplace grievances, rant about colleagues, or reveal employee-employer disputes through social channels. Such acts not only invite unwelcome drama but also denote a flagrant lack of professional judgment.

8.3. Engage, Don't Enrage

While social media platforms are interactive arenas nurturing dialogue and discourse, they can quickly transform into battlegrounds of conflicting opinions. Stay poised, do not engage in inflammatory debates or aggressive confrontations. Instead, practice thoughtful and respectful responses.

Several conversation threads are bait for online trolls. Recognize them and avoid falling into those traps. Block, report, or disengage from users and conversations that threaten your online peace and professional reputation. Remember, every digital footprint is permanent.

8.4. Networking and Building Relationships

In a world condensed by Internet connectivity, social media has emerged as a potent networking tool. Interact with your industry peers, participate in discussions, share ideas, or even celebrate achievements. Compliment others genuinely and extend support when someone strives for it. Value the 'social' in the media and make authenticity the cornerstone of your networking efforts.

Professionals often underestimate the unrivaled potential of LinkedIn, a networking platform designed exclusively for professional collaborations. Build a robust profile, keep it up to date, join relevant groups and interact actively. Regularly share knowledgeable content relevant to your industry, which can position you as a thought leader.

8.5. Dos and Don'ts of Social Media Etiquette

Here, we present a succinct list of paramount dos and don'ts to guide you through the social media maze:

DOs: - Do consistently maintain an active and relevant online presence. - Do use respectful, courteous language. - Do practice meticulous discretion in sharing. - Do connect, communicate and engage constructively. - Do value, respect and understand diverse viewpoints.

DON'Ts: - Don't overshare or disclose confidential information. - Don't engage in inflammatory, aggressive discourse. - Don't forget that every post contributes to your digital persona. - Don't underestimate the power of perception. - Don't overlook the immense potential of networking in the professional arena.

Circling back to where we begun, harnessing the power of social media requires respecting its responsibility. Understand the infinite reverberations of every word and every click. Respect digital spaces as living ecosystems mirroring societal norms and professional courtesies. Remember always, a screen and a keyboard do not provide immunity against accountability. Let's pledge to exercise mature judgment and forethought. After all, the digital age is here to stay, and so too, the art of being respectfully social in it.

Chapter 9. Cross-Cultural Etiquette: Navigating the Global Business Landscape

In an era of increasing globalization, businesses find themselves regularly interacting with partners, clients, and colleagues from a dizzying array of cultures and countries. For those of us focused on business success, it becomes paramount to understand, appreciate, and adapt to the vastly varying cultural expectations and social mores that we may encounter across continents. This chapter delves into a deep exploration of cross-cultural etiquette, serving as your guide to aptly maneuver the multifarious and intricate global business terrain.

9.1. The Importance of Cross-Cultural Understanding

In the past, business was predominantly local, and most interactions and transactions were conducted with people of the same or similar cultural backgrounds. But the growing trend of globalization has changed all that, necessitating the capacity to connect and communicate effectively with members of distinct cultures. Failure to cultivate cultural awareness and sensitivity can result in miscommunication, strained relationships, damaged reputations, and in turn, lost business opportunities.

Take the example of a US-based software firm that, in its eagerness to expand into the Asian market, failed to conduct adequate cultural research. It made numerous faux pas, from business attire to negotiation tactics, ultimately resulting in the loss of multiple promising partnerships. Situations like these underline the dire need for businesses to become adept in the artistry of cross-cultural communication and etiquette.

9.2. Understanding Cultural Differences: The Key to Global Success

Starting a discussion about cultural differences, it's important to recognize that cultures are not monoliths. They showcase a remarkable diversity in terms of beliefs, values, traditions, social norms, communication styles, and practices. What may be perfectly acceptable and professional in one culture, may be viewed as offensive or inappropriate in another. Therefore, to effectively navigate the global business plain, it's indispensable to understand these cultural variances and their impact on business interactions.

A nutshell illustration of such a scenario may shed more light. Picture a business gathering involving professionals from Germany, Japan, and Brazil. The German is likely to value punctuality, directness, and clear, structured communication. The Japanese counterpart may prioritize harmony, indirect expressions, and the minutiae of ceremony. The Brazilian might bring a sense of friendliness, relaxed attitudes towards time, and comfortable physical contact. You can imagine the potential for misunderstanding in such a constellation, elucidating the importance of understanding and respecting cultural disparities.

9.3. Developing Cross-Cultural Competencies

The journey towards developing cross-cultural competencies is much like venturing into a dense forest. One must carry the right tools — in the form of informational resources and learning methods, the correct mindset — embodying adaptability and respect, and a guiding light — the desire to build successful cross-cultural relationships.

Ideally, becoming adept at cross-cultural communication begins with research and self-education. This can involve books, online resources, consultation with cultural advisers, or attending cultural training seminars. An effective technique is to learn the native language, providing a deeper perspective into the cultural context.

Next, it's important to develop behavioral flexibility, which means modifying one's behavior, communication style, and type of interactions to match the cultural environment. It also demands being observant and receptive to non-verbal cues, which often carry hefty cultural significance.

Lastly, harboring a respectful and empathetic attitude towards cultural diversity is vital. Respect others' traditions, rituals, and customs, and celebrate the diversity they introduce into our global business landskip.

9.4. Making Mistakes and Learning From Them

Nobody is perfect, and it's entirely possible that you will make some cultural faux pas while navigating the unfamiliar terrains of international business dynamics. What matters the most, however, is how you react and learn from these inadvertent mistakes. Acknowledge your blunders candidly, make amends if necessary, learn what went wrong, and forge forward equipped with a new understanding.

9.5. Conclusion: Embracing Diversity in Global Business

In conclusion, cross-cultural etiquette is a critical skill in today's globalized business world. It involves understanding unique customs, adopting the appropriate demeanor, embracing diversity, and having the humility to learn from mistakes. The treacherous waves of cultural differences may pull you down momentarily, but they'll also endow you with the strength to swim in the vast ocean of global business possibilities.

Success in the global arena is not just about your business acumen; it's also about your understanding of the world at large. And truly, isn't that a more enriching way of conducting business after all? The descent into the world of diverse cultures may seem daunting, yet it ultimately empowers you to metamorphose into a more competent, global business professional, enabling you to catalyze profound bonds and seal rewarding business deals across the globe. Grasp the essence of cross-cultural dynamics and let your business flourish in the vivid tapestry of the worldwide landscape!

Chapter 10. Overcoming Communication Barriers: A Pathway to Effective Conversation

In a world shaped by an avalanche of information and buffeted by incessant communication, one of the biggest challenges facing professionals today is the omnipresent risk of communication barriers. Imagine yourself in the shoes of someone facing these barriers on a daily basis. It's akin to driving a car without a roadmap. Every twist and turn, every halt and hurry, they all become rather unpredictable, affecting the overall effectiveness of your journey. Overcoming these barriers doesn't just become important—it becomes indispensable. Engage now in an intensive exploration of these barriers and the pathways to effective conversation that ameliorate their impact in the landscape of professional communication.

10.1. Unraveling Communication Barriers

The story of overcoming communication barriers begins with understanding them. They flaunt various guises and operate at several levels. Anything that compromises the clarity, accuracy, and effectiveness of a communication can be categorized as a communication barrier.

Physical barriers, for instance, are often underestimated. Distances between team members, obstructions like walls and doors, or even technological issues such as poor audio or video quality can tarnish communication.

Then we have psychological or emotional barriers. Fear, mistrust, or apathy can make participants less receptive, causing messages to be diluted or misinterpreted. Cultural and language differences can also pose formidable barriers, particularly in diverse, global teams.

Finally, we encounter systemic barriers found within the organizational structure. Unwritten rules, politics, power dynamics, information hoarding—these may all impair the free-flowing exchange of ideas and thoughts.

10.2. Breaking Down the Barriers

Tackling these barriers requires a combination of knowledge, adaptability, and proactivity. Let's delve into the multitude of measures you can implement to overcome these challenges.

Firstly, it's crucial to maintain a clear, precise, and coherent communication style. Being deliberate about what you say, how you say it, and when you say it can prevent misunderstandings. Using plain language, avoiding jargon, and not assuming the receiver's knowledge of the subject contributes substantially to clarity.

Active listening goes hand in hand with clear communication. Many communication barriers arise because messages are not heard or understood the way they should be. Effective listeners don't just hear; they interpret, understand, and respond thoughtfully.

Within multicultural teams, embracing cultural diversity can help overcome barriers. Seek to understand cultural nuances, preferences, and taboos. Learn phrases in other languages, develop an understanding of different communication styles, and value diverse opinions.

Technological tools also play a significant role in balancing physical distances. Employing the right audio-visual equipment, collaboration tools, and technology platforms can bridge gaps. Moreover, maintaining a response rhythm can mitigate the time gap caused by different time zones.

Psychological barriers can be addressed by creating a safe and supportive environment. Fostering inclusivity, acknowledging contributions, encouraging open conversations, and demonstrating vulnerability are a recipe for a harmonious communication ecosystem.

Lastly, systemic barriers necessitate structural changes. Cultivating a transparent culture, encouraging desiloization, and developing open channels of communication can disintegrate these barriers.

10.3. Establishing a Barrier-Free Communication Culture

In the context of organizational communication, overcoming barriers isn't solely an individual responsibility. It requires a collective effort, a shared commitment to creating a barrier-free communication culture.

Establishing such a culture emphasizes building a foundation of trust. Openness fosters honest communication, with diverse perspectives treated respectfully. Active listening becomes the norm, not the exception.

In this new culture, employees are trained not just to receive information, but to seek answers too. It encourages participants to question assumptions, check understanding, respond constructively, and provide comprehensive feedback.

This culture manifests itself both in formal, structured settings and in the casual watercooler chats. Every conversation is an opportunity to foster inclusivity, diversity, and mutual respect.

As you reinvent your communication culture, remember that change is a process, not an event. It takes time, effort, and a whole lot of conversation. Persist beyond the challenges, and you'll be met with communication success beyond measure.

10.4. A Pathway Paved with Opportunities

From the simplest conversations to the most convoluted discourses, breaking down barriers can illuminate the path to effective communication in profound ways. This journey isn't always easy, but it's undeniably rewarding.

Once you overcome these barriers, opportunities unfold. Collaboration strengthens, relationships deepen, ideas flow more freely, and productivity soars. The very fabric of your professional life changes as you weave it with efficiency, effectiveness, and empathy.

In essence, the process of overcoming communication barriers redefines the way you engage with your profession and stakeholders. It empowers you, liberates you, and charts a course of sustainability for competent communication—your passport to professional success.

This expedition through the landscape of communication barriers and the route to overcoming them propels us towards the zenith of professional communication. Harness these insights and transform your communication, one conversation at a time. As you negate these barriers, you don't merely survive the professional wilderness—you thrive in it.

Chapter 11. Conclusion: Reaping the Benefits of Professional Communication and Etiquette

As we arrive at the final point of our comprehensive investigation into the intricacies of business etiquette and professional communication, it's time to harvest the fruits of the knowledge acquired thus far. Throughout our expedition, we've studied the ways in which communication impacts various aspects of business, from interpersonal relationships to strategic advantages. It's now time to perceptively appraise the advantages of incorporating strong communication skills and business etiquette into your professional repertoire.

11.1. The Impact on Business Relationships

In the corporate arena, relationships are the solid bedrock upon which enduring success is anchored, largely influenced by effective communication. Thoughtful conversation, active listening, professional correspondence, and accurate interpreting of non-verbal cues can establish and nurture positive professional relationships. Employing etiquette can express your respect and consideration for others, fostering a nurturing and harmonious environment conducive to cooperation and productivity. It's an investment in social capital, yielding high dividends in the form of stronger alliances, enhanced collaboration, increased trust, and collective success.

11.2. Increasing Personal Brand Value

Unimpeachable business etiquette and competent communication tend to infuse an aura of sophistication and professionalism to your persona. They can serve as key components of your personal branding strategy, helping you stand out in competitive settings. You may soon find yourself being sought after for advice, collaborations, or leadership roles, having established yourself as a respectful, cultured, and articulate professional. It's a monumental step towards self-fulfillment and career growth in today's fast-paced business landscape.

11.3. Facilitation of Operational Efficiency

Smooth workflow is the lifeblood of organizational efficiency. Crisp, clear, and courteous communication promotes better understanding, reduces misinterpretations, and mitigates friction, keeping the gears of productivity in motion. Etiquette punctuates this interplay with a tone of respect, paving the way for a smooth, conflict-free work environment. Combining both can help streamline operations and enhance efficiency by ensuring that instructions, feedback, and information are accurately conveyed and received.

11.4. Enhancing Cross-Cultural Relations

In an era where globalization and digital communication have brought businesses closer, cross-cultural interactions are not just commonplace but necessary. Knowledge of business etiquette and effective communication can ensure you navigate this multi-cultural landscape more diplomatically. Appreciating different communication styles, business customs, or societal norms can forge stronger international relationships and facilitate smoother negotiations.

11.5. Bridging the Gap through Conflict Resolution

Conflicts, if left unattended, can threaten the very fabric of a smooth working environment. Skilled communication combined with sound business etiquette can serve as a bridge to resolve conflicts and restore harmony. By treating each party with respect, promoting open dialogue, and actively listening to grievances, you contribute to an environment conducive to problem-solving.

11.6. Rising Through the Leadership Ladder

Effective communication and eloquent etiquette are crucial skills for those aspiring to leadership roles. Leaders need to inspire trust, command respect, and foster teamwork - all of which are considerably more manageable with polished communication and etiquette. You not only set a positive example but also exercise a benign influence on your team's behavior and attitude.

To sum it all up, the wisdom you've gained from this report isn't just about adhering to certain protocols or selecting the right words. It's about reshaping your professional identity, fostering relationships, and positioning yourself favorably in the global business sphere. It's about creating a realm where respect, understanding, and collaboration reign supreme. With practice and patience, the seeds of professional etiquette and communication that you've sowed will grow into a rich harvest, transforming not just your professional standing but your personal life too, paving the way for an exciting, fulfilling journey up the corporate ladder.

www.ingramcontent.com/pod-product-compliance
Lightning Source LLC
Chambersburg PA
CBHW062306290526
45794CB00006B/2710